GARY LLOYD NOLAND
COLLECTED PIANO WORKS
VOLUME 2

7TH SPECIES PUBLICATIONS

13080 Princeton Court, Lake Oswego OR 97035

email: nolandgary5@gmail.com

website: https://composergarynoland.godaddysites.com/

Published by 7th Species
13080 Princeton Court
Lake Oswego OR 97035

Composer's website: https://composergarynoland.godaddysites.com/

Contact email: nolandgary5@gmail.com

ISBN/SKU: 978-1-7323023-9-6

First printed 2021

Title page and all interior illustrations by Lon Gaylord Dylan (the composer's visual artist alter ego).

Also by GARY LLOYD NOLAND

Books

COLLECTED PIANO WORKS: Volume 1

JAGDLIED: a Chamber Novel for Narrator, Musicians, Pantomimists, Dancers & Culinary Artists

NOTHING IS MORE: a High Black Comedy in Verse with Music for Six Actors

Music CDs

Available from NorthPacificMusic.com:

SELECTED MUSIC FROM VENGE ART
ROYAL OILWORKS MUSIC
24 INTERLUDES FOR PIANO OP. 71, VOL. 1
24 INTERLUDES FOR PIANO OP. 71, VOL. 2
24 POSTLUDES FOR PIANO OP. 72, VOL. 1
24 POSTLUDES FOR PIANO OP. 72, VOL. 2

in collaboration with other composers:

PASSION
PLAYERLESS PIANOS

Available from 7th Species (https://composergarynoland.godaddysites.com/)

20 COVIDITTIES OP. 116 (double CD)
ENTROPIC ABANDON (double CD)
MUSIC OF RAGE, SORROW, LOVE, LAUGHTER & BUREAUCRACY (double CD, release pending)
DISSONAPHOBIC FEVER DREAMS Op. 118
STATE-OF-THE-ART EAR EXERCISES FOR MUSICAL COGNOSCENTI Op. 119
WAYWARD AFFECTS & AFFLICTIONS Op. 120

MUSIC SCORES

Multiple scores available from Freeland (7th Species) Publications, J.W. Pepper, Sheet Music Plus, RGM

COMPOSER'S NOTES

One of the most ambitious sets of solo piano variations in the keyboard literature, Noland's 39 VARIATIONS ON AN ORIGINAL THEME IN F MAJOR Op. 98 (2009-2011) awaits its world premiere at the time of this writing (7 September, 2021), well over a decade subsequent to its completion on 10 July, 2011. A tolerably decent mechanical rendition of the entire opus may be heard at the following link (in two segments): https://soundcloud.com/gary-noland/sets/39-variations-on-an-original-1

Ragtime pianist Mark Lutton once described Noland's GRANDE RAG BRILLANTE Op. 15 as "the most difficult ragtime piece of all time … The audience needs to have Attention Hyperabundance Disorder. (It's fine if, like me, your idea of a nice short little piece is a tone poem by Richard Strauss.)" The Canadian pianist and composer Max Keelyside described it as "the work of a musician's musician." GRANDE RAG BRILLANTE received its official world premiere on KPFA Radio on 4 October, 1991 in celebration of the inauguration of Pacifica Radio's (then) sparkling new facility in Berkeley, California. It was "performed" on a computer-driven Yamaha Disklavier. This historic premiere, paired with the world premiere of a (then) new work by Lou Harrison, was later written up in Nicolas Slonimsky's celebrated book MUSIC SINCE 1900 (an encyclopedic compendium that chronologically lists premieres of compositions that its author deems to be among the most significant and noteworthy of the twentieth century). American composer Ernesto Ferreri wrote of this work, "Only a musical maniac could push something this far … at times the rags fugue and the fugues rag into waves of improbable climaxes … noticed a double fugue with the rag theme … and you gotta love how it detours around atonality … brillante indeed!" The late Slovak composer and conductor Ladislav Kupkovic (1936-2016) once wrote to Noland: "…*Ihre Musik ist wunderschön, 'Grande Rag Brillante' ist ein Meisterwerk; als auch Komponist bin ich voll Neid, dass ich so etwas nicht schreiben kann. Ich wünsche Ihnen viel Erfolg! Ich komponiere schon viele Jahre europäisch tonal und es ist nicht leicht, so zu komponieren in einer Welt, die noch in der atonalen Ideologie denkt. Ich hoffe, Ihr Weg wird leichter…*" Spoiler Alert: It hasn't been. Here is a link to a computer-driven performance of GRANDE RAG BRILLANTE on a Yamaha Disklavier piano: https://soundcloud.com/gary-noland/grande-rag-brillante-for-piano-op-15 This recording is included on the CD compilation of compositions by Noland titled "Selected Music from Venge Art," which is available for purchase at: http:// www.northpacificmusic.com/VengeArt.html

GOLDEN GATE RAG Op. 123 was originally sketched out (read: composed) in 1974, just a little over a year after Noland started taking piano/composition lessons from one of the Bay Area's leading musicians, the brilliant and eccentric polymath Goodwin Sammel (1925-2020), in Berkeley, California at the relatively ripened age (as compared with many of his immensely more privileged peers) of sixteen following a lengthy sojourn (1970-72) in Western Europe, much of the time spent in Salzburg (birthplace of Mozart) and Garmisch-Partenkirchen (home of Richard Strauss) with virtually no access to a piano. A fast learner and fiercely motivated, by the time he had reached his seventeenth year, while still only in high school, Noland had acquired a singularly extraordinary command of tonal (i.e., common practice) harmony for one with as scant a musical training as he had thus far had, and in despite of his having been raised in a semi-dysfunctional broken home in an excessively combative and unsupportive environment. He attributes this natural comprehension of the musical language in part to the collective unconscious of the cultural background of his forebears (he was raised in a family of German Jewish Holocaust survivors who had been forced into exile by the Nazis) as well as to the fact that his father (who had separated from his mother when Noland was only two years of age) was a master chess player and professor of mathematics. Even more so, however, he attributes it to his own fanatical focus and almost superhuman patience in attempting to solve complex musico-technical (i.e., voice-leading and structural) problems in his formative compositional exertions. Noland's uncommon technical proficiency in the tonal language gave him a competitive edge over many of his fellow students and professors in both college and graduate school, which was, most probably, one of the root causes of the intense friction between him and certain of his teachers and colleagues who were dyed-in-the-wool academic modernists (hence indifferent to functional harmony and, moreover, insecure in their own astonishingly limited command thereof). A heretofore unpublished and newly revised version of Golden Gate Rag (completed in August, 2021) is included in this collection.

THREE MEDLEYS comprise a series of strung-together musical excerpts from various works by Richard Strauss, Mahler, Korngold, Schönberg, Berg, Beethoven, J.S. Bach, Brahms, Karol Szymanowski, Mozart, and Hugo Wolf. These satirical Medleys are excerpted from Fascicles #3 (Op. 45), #4 (Op. 49), and #5 (Op. 54) of Noland's heretofore unfinished 150-hour long chamber novel VENGE ART (a musico-literary Gesamtkunstwerk with a strong visual artistic component, which the composer embarked upon in 1994 with unrelenting ferocity, and which remains, to this very hour, a work in progress).

The musical material of THREE INCONGRUISMS Op. 122 (2021) is derived from various unfinished compositions dating back to the late 1970s and mid 1980s. These sketches were only recently revised and are published here for the first time.

TABLE OF CONTENTS

GARY NOLAND

39 VARIATIONS

on an Original Theme in F Major

for solo piano

Op. 98

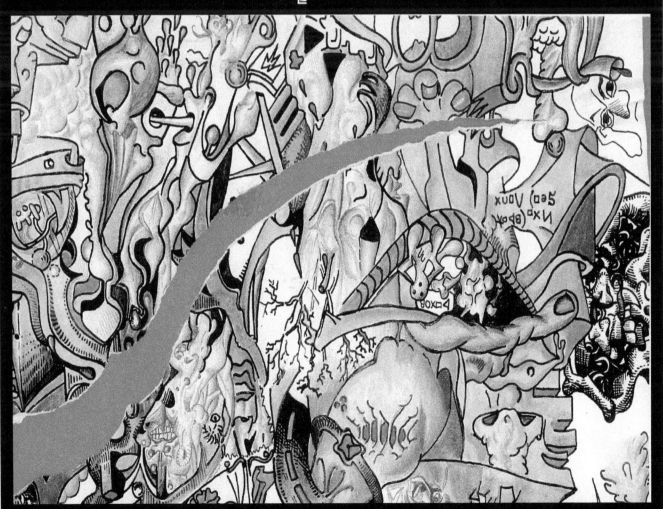

Freeland Publications

PREFACE

I began composing this piece in April 2009 and completed it on July 10th, 2011. During this period, I came up with many titles for it. My first idea, inspired by the worldwide "Great Recession," was to call it *The Geltschmerz Variations*. Over time, however, such a title seemed frivolous in light of how important this work was to my oeuvre. Another brainstorm that hit me was to name it after my favorite hiking trail in the city where I reside (Portland, Oregon), to wit: *The Wildwood Variations*. Such a title, however, exudes an unpleasant odor of provincialism. At one point, when I considered the travails suffered in the process of composing this piece (having lived on borrowed time while doing so), I decided to call it *Forty Minus One Variations*. This title, however, conjures up images of torturers wielding whips and whatnot. Other titles I considered were: *Misanthropic Variations, Quixotic Variations, Ecstatic Variations, Suicidal Variations, The Diarrhea Variations, The People Defeated Will Never Be United*, and so on. Many of these titles seemed unjustifiably cynical and most of them either rang hollow or failed to resonate with the spirit of the piece.

I don't know, ... I might eventually have to give in to my baser instincts and permit this opus to be taken for some unter-species of parochial *Genericana* and, come hell or high water, gnash my teeth on my way to the bank. All seriousness aside, perhaps I'll just go ahead and name it after my favorite stomping ground in Portland-a cafe on NW Thurman Street-and dutifully christen it *The Saint Honore Variations* ... (Fat chance!)

After mulling over my various options, I decided in the end to stick to the time-honored practice of conferring upon this opus a bland and neutral title, which lends to it, I suppose, a certain gravitas and/or *je ne sais quoi*. Even so, I may assent to future musicologists devising a nickname for it, should they plot to do so. As far as I can determine, at the time of this writing, this is the *biggest*, if not the *baddest*, set of solo piano variations in the history of the genre, far surpassing in scope Bach's Goldberg Variations, Beethoven's Diabelli Variations, and Frederic Rzewski's variations on Sergio Ortega's anthem. *¡El pueblo unido, jamas sera vencido!*. An informant tipped me off that Kaikhosru Shapurgi Sorabji (aka Leon Dudley) may have written some larger sets (possibly based on passacaglia ostinati), but I have yet to stumble upon them. Suffice to say, it is my fervent hope that I will be able to hang on long enough to hear my own set performed by a well-qualified super-virtuoso.

Gary Noland
Portland Oregon
July 11th, 2011

NOTES

Unless otherwise indicated, all trills, long and short, are to begin on the upper auxiliary. The small squiggles(⌇) seen throughout this score should not be interpreted as inverted mordants but rather as short trills (generally two or three shakes starting on the upper note) as described in Bach's Table of Ornaments.

*　　*　　*

Please note that a wide range of interpretations of this piece is possible. My indications of dynamics, tempos, articulations, and phrasings may be viewed as general guidelines and should not, therefore, be construed as being "carved in stone." Pianists are encouraged to be flexible in their interpretations of this score and are hence advised not to take its performance markings too literally. It is imperative, notwithstanding, that those who make bold to perform this piece should do so with unrelenting focus, unflinching determination, and unwavering faith in their musical convictions.

Gary Noland
Portland Oregon
July 11th, 2011

39 Variations
on an Original Theme in F Major
for solo piano

by Gary Noland, Op. 98

Thema

Andante con moto (♩ = ca. 118—126)

Var.1
L'istesso tempo

Var.2

L'istesso tempo

Var.3

Meno mosso

*All trills begin on the upper auxiliary.

11

13

15

22

poco rit. - a tempo

28

Var.11
Larghetto mit Ernst, Strenge und Feierlichkeit

31

Var.12
Allegretto luminoso; con estasi
♩ = ca. 100-106

Var.13
Allegretto elegantemente;
avec noblesse

♩ = ca. 96-108

41

56

60

62

63

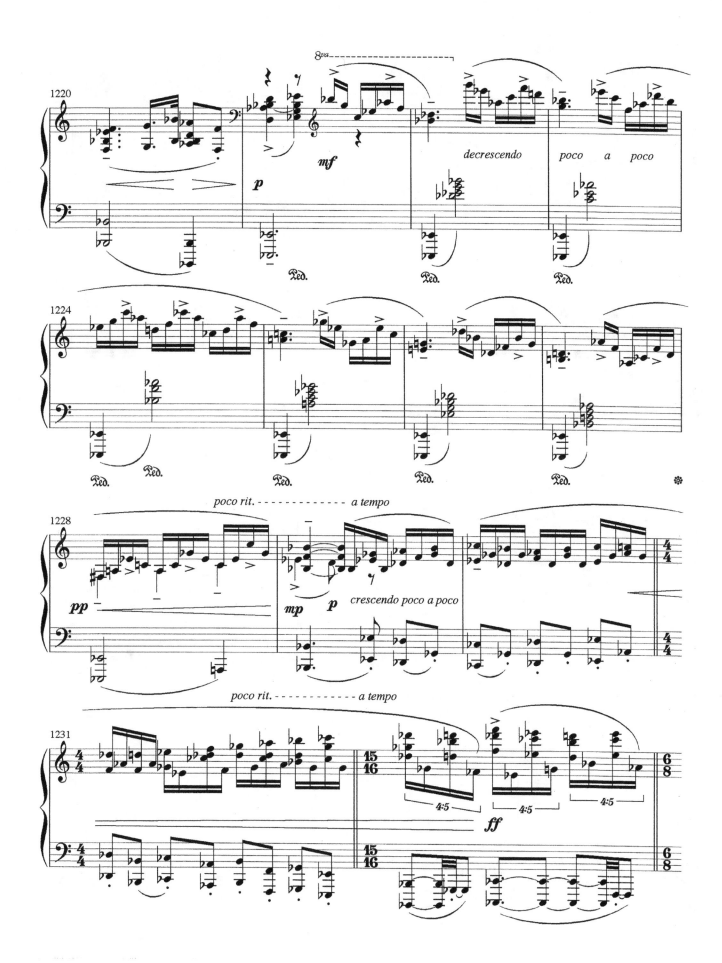

65

Var.20
Andante con moto; streng

73

Var.23
Andante; un poco rubato

♩ = ca. 64-76

Var.24
Adagietto con gravità

poco rit. - - - - - - - - a tempo

91

99

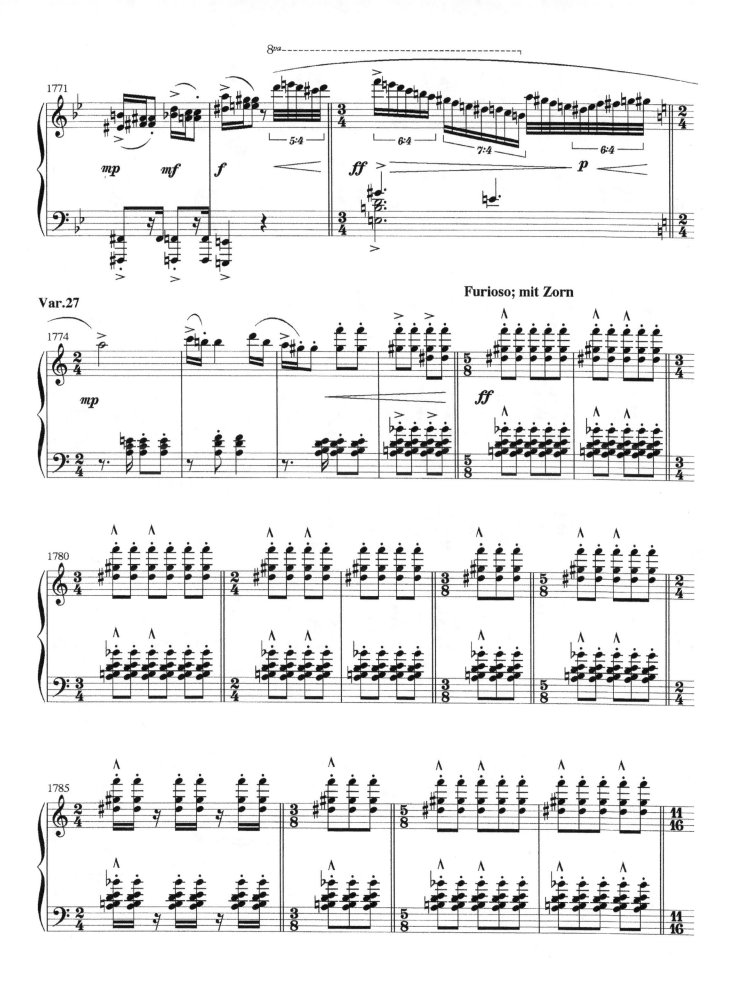

Var.27

Furioso; mit Zorn

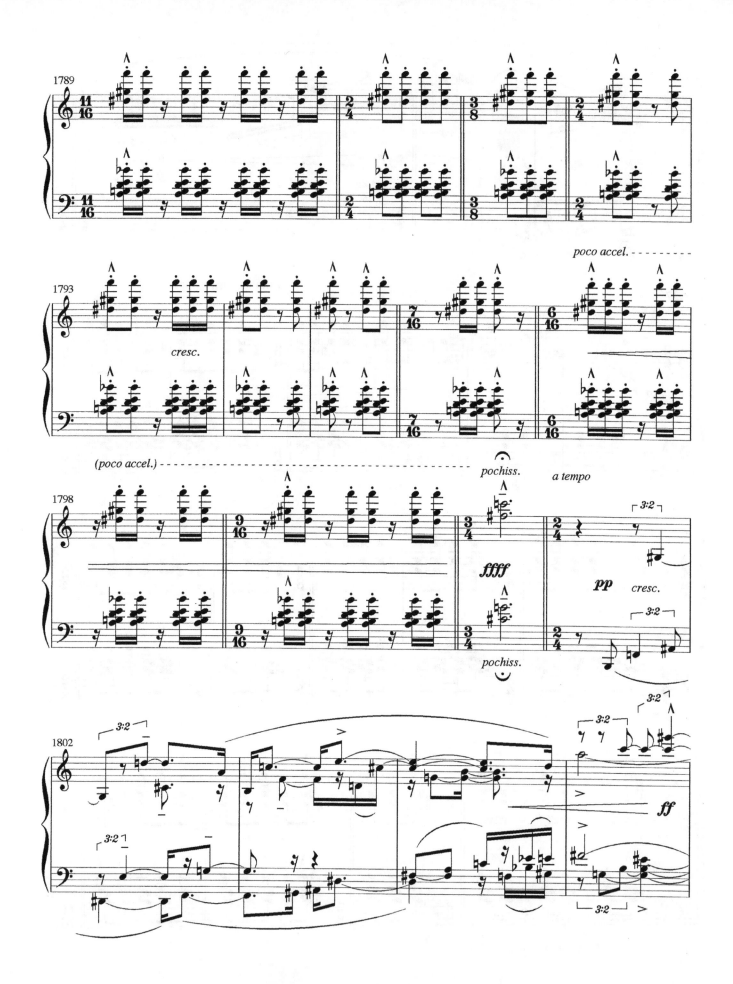

*Sustain chords in upper register with sostenuto pedal.

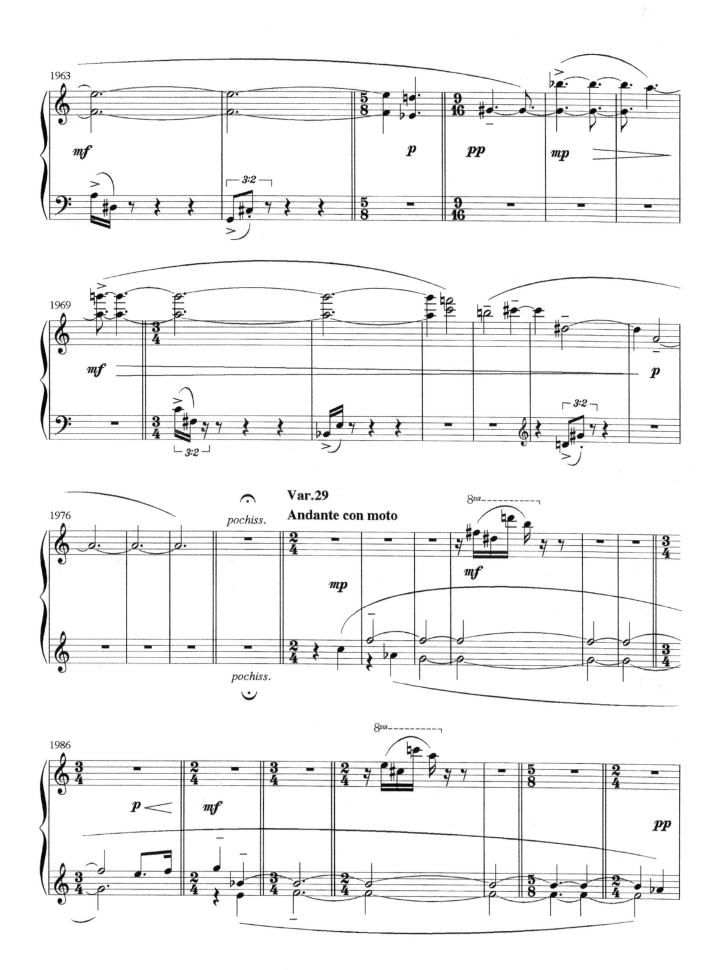

117

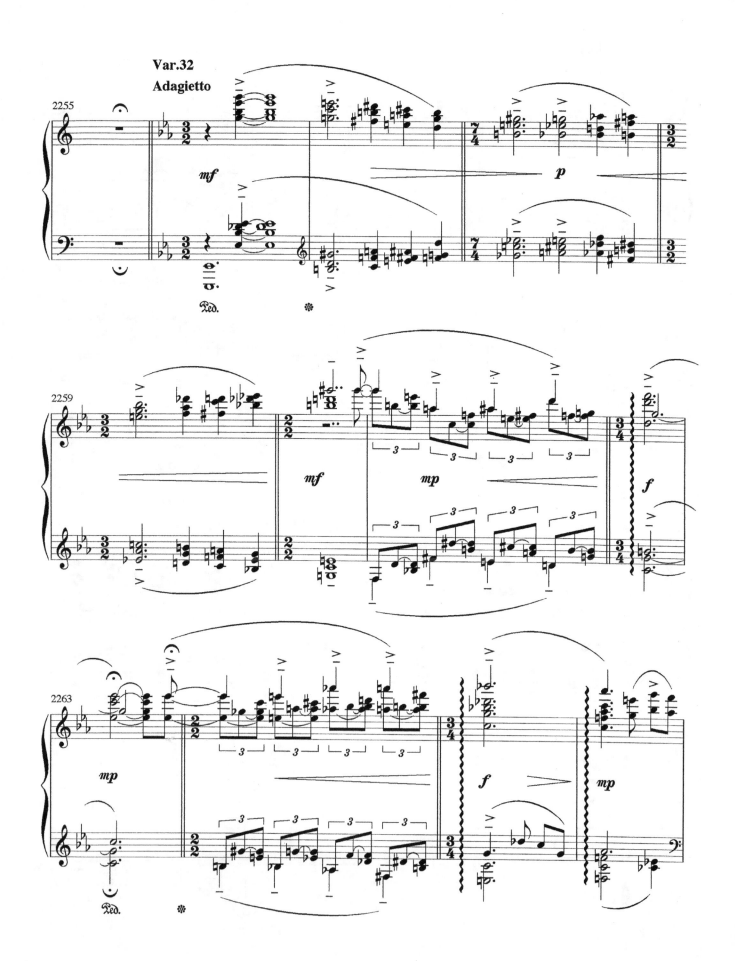

133

135

Like marzipan

138

139

141

150

153

166

Var.38
Speak softly and carry a big stick …

172

176

177

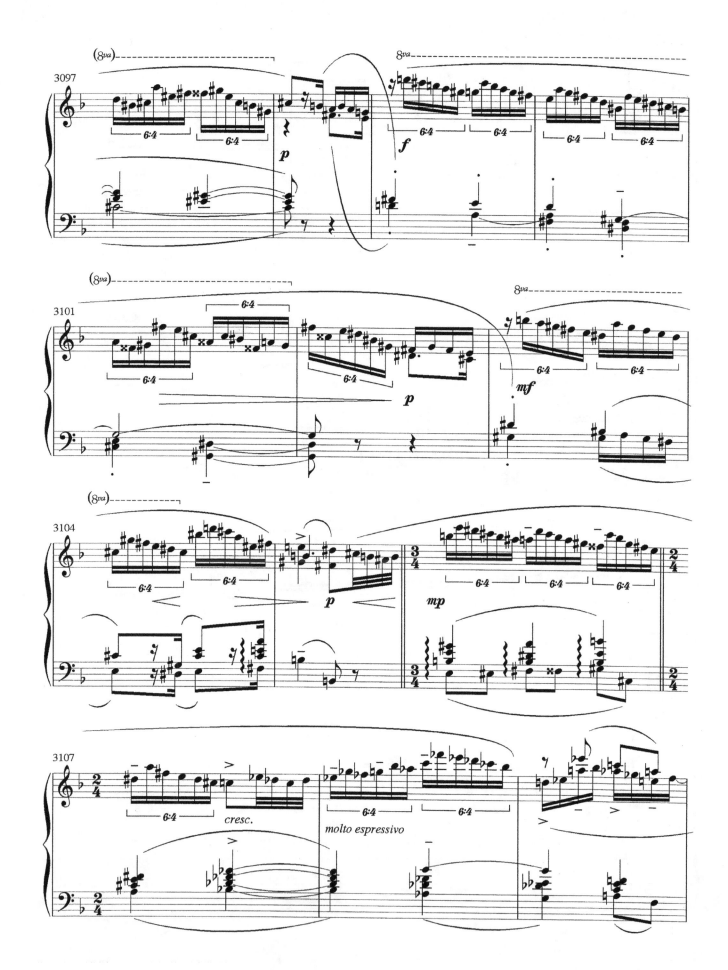

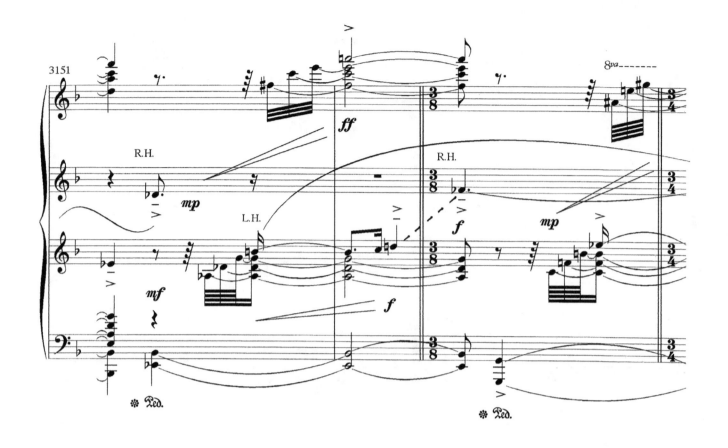

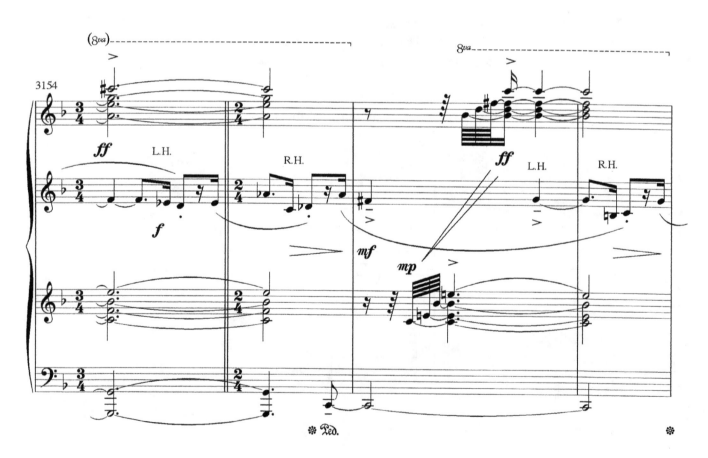

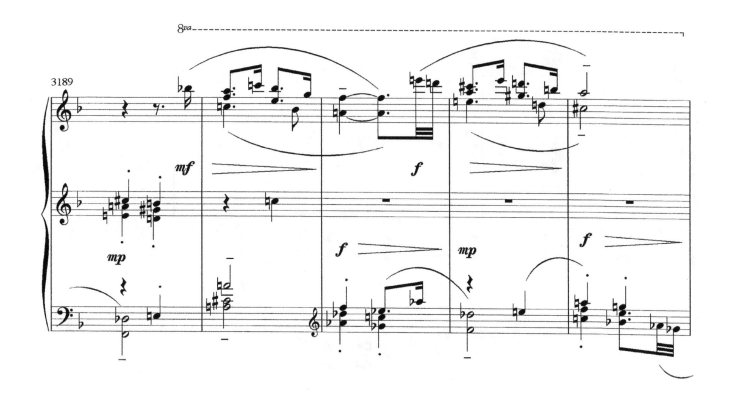

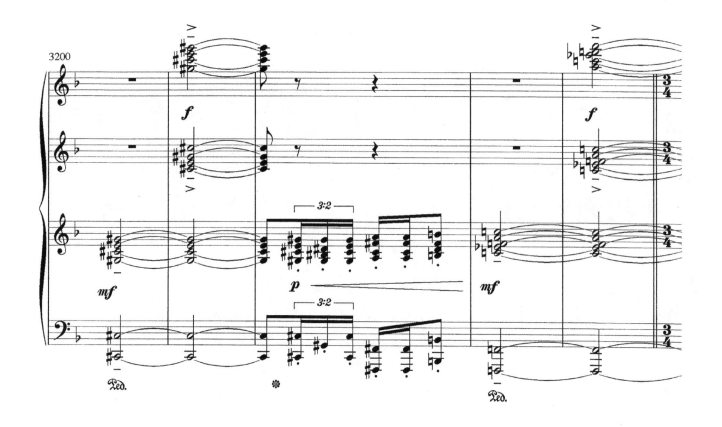

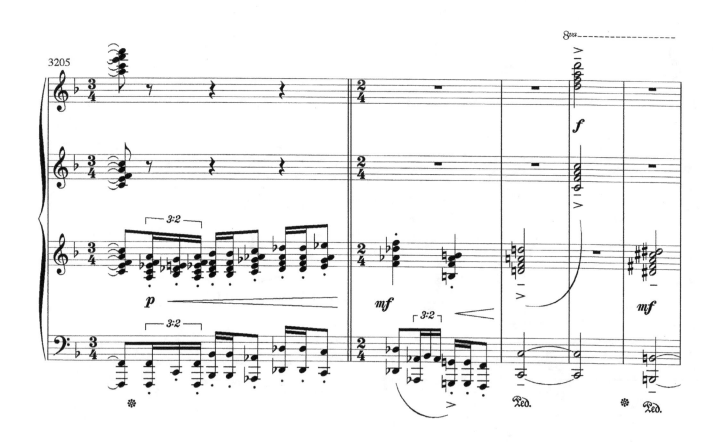

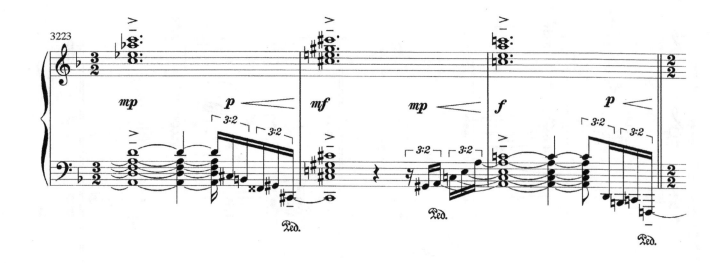

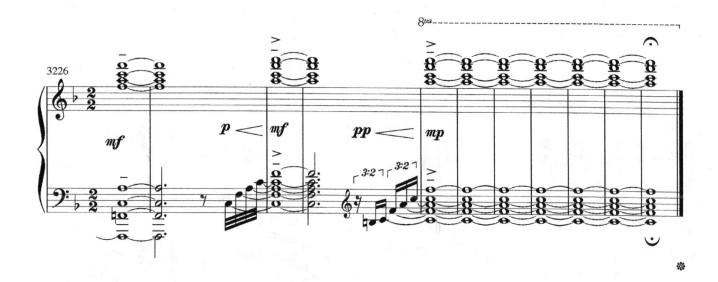

"Grande Rag Brillante"

for piano

Op. 15, by Gary Noland
(composed 1979; recomposed 1989)

dedicated to
Charles Amirkhanian

* record-player-turntable-change-of-speed effect.

196

162
mf
166
mp
169
173
mf
poco rit.
mp
R.H.
(♩= ca. 83)
177
L.H.
poco accel.
L.H.
R.H.

202

Tempo I, with brute force!

205

211

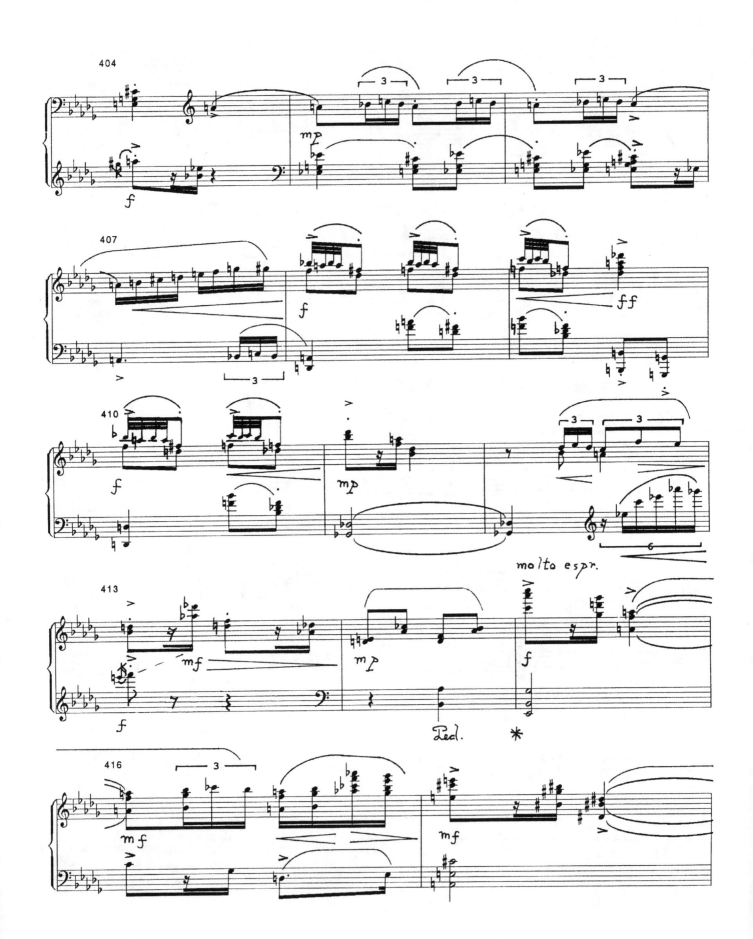

218

219

220

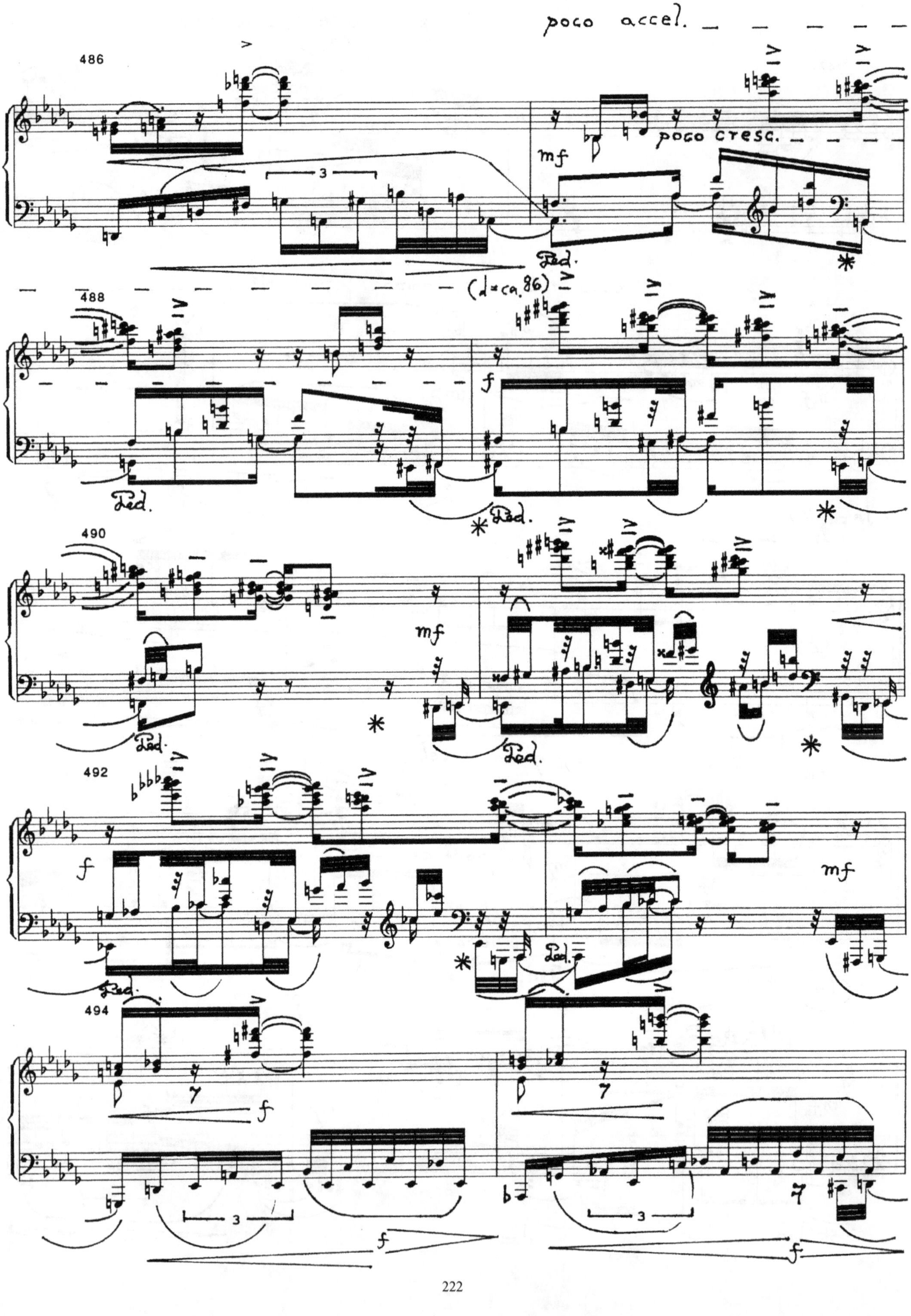
poco accel.
486
poco cresc.
mf
(♩= ca. 86)
488
f
490
mf
492
f
mf
494
f
f
f

223

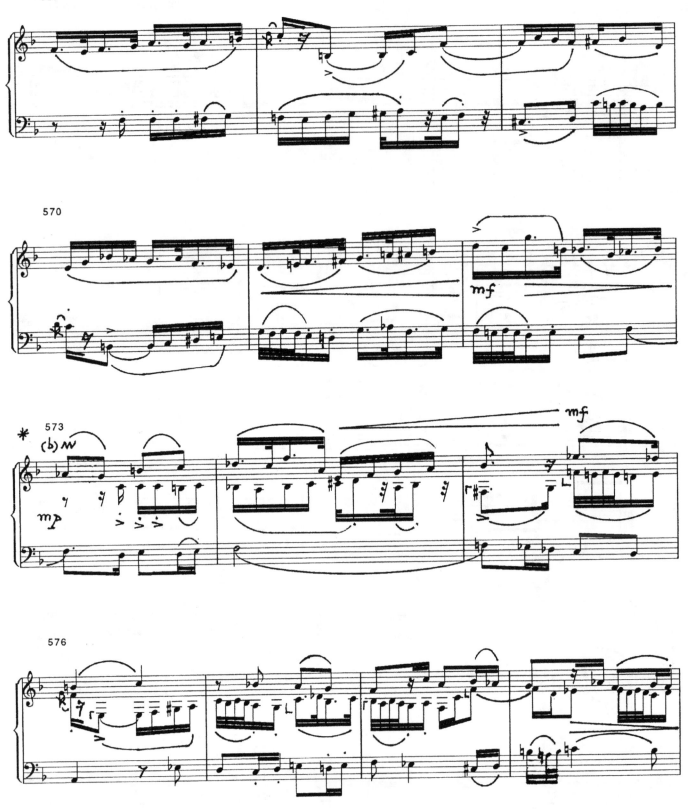

* start trill on main note.

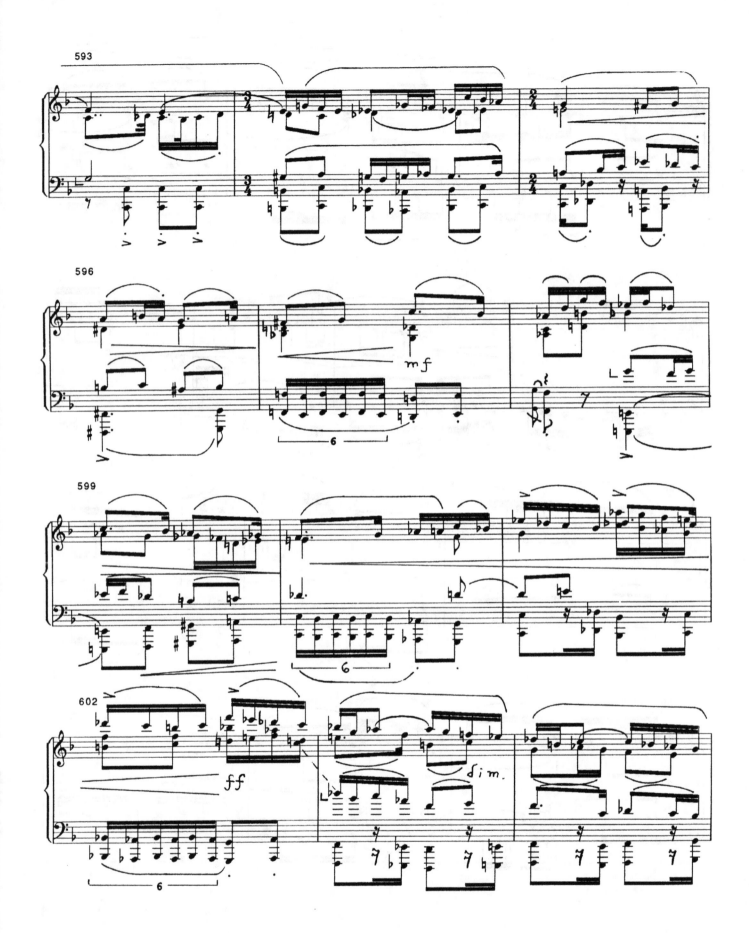

233

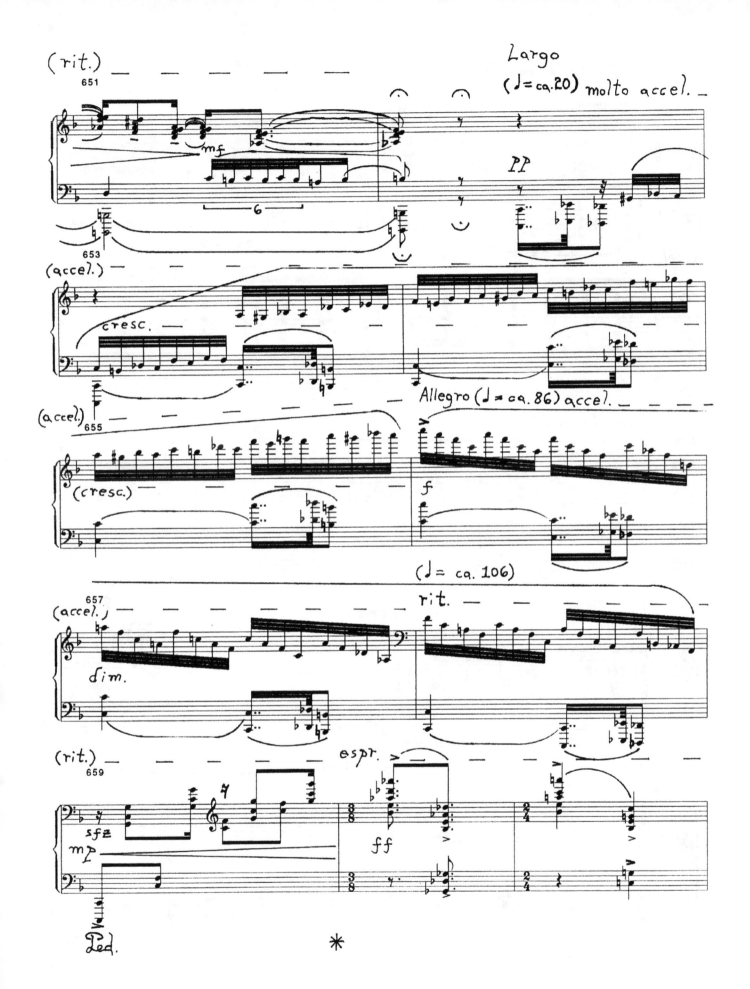

235

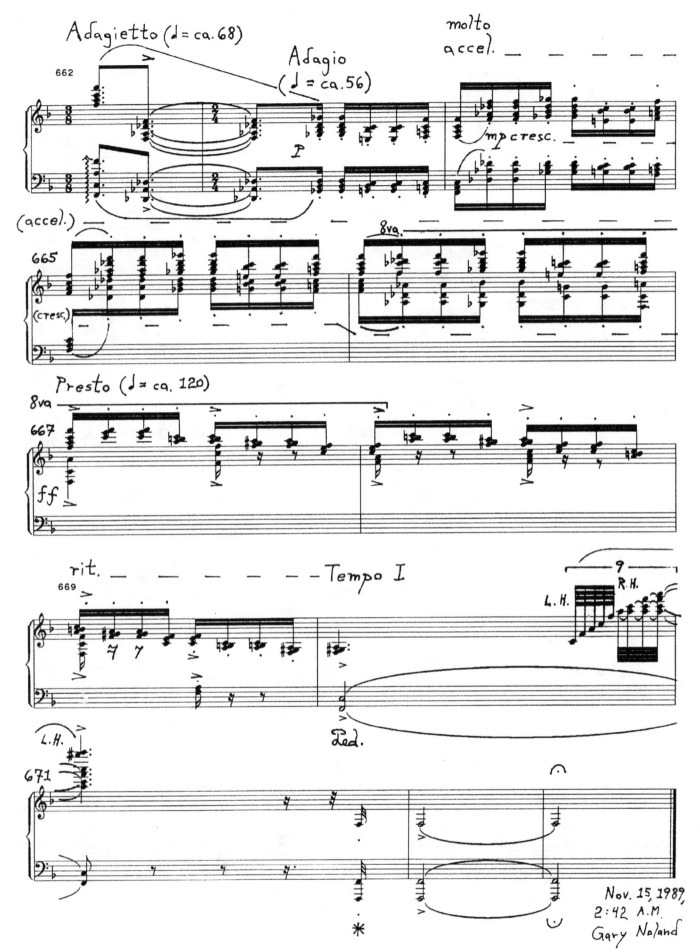

236

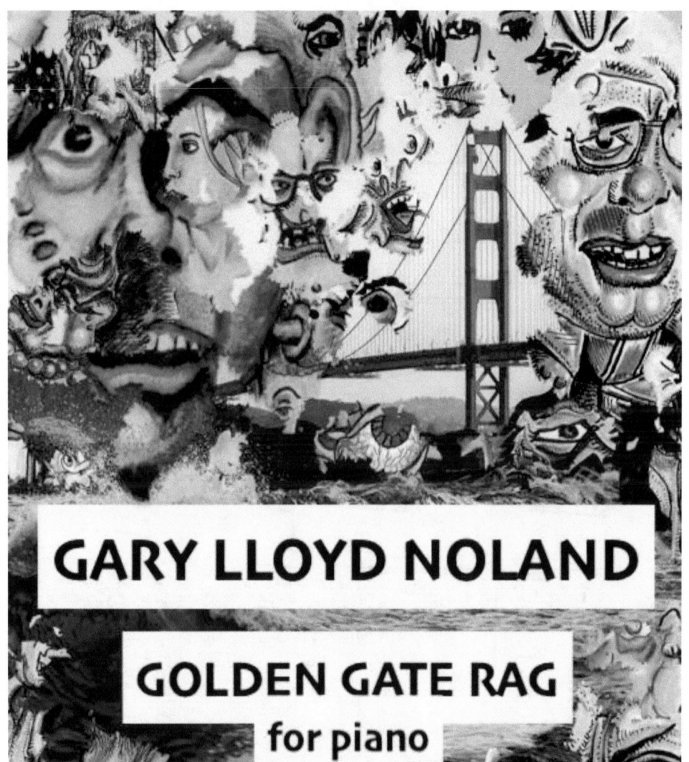

GARY LLOYD NOLAND

GOLDEN GATE RAG
for piano

Op. 123

GOLDEN GATE RAG

for piano

in memoriam Victor Steinhardt (1943-2021)

Gary Lloyd Noland, Op. 123

238

241

244

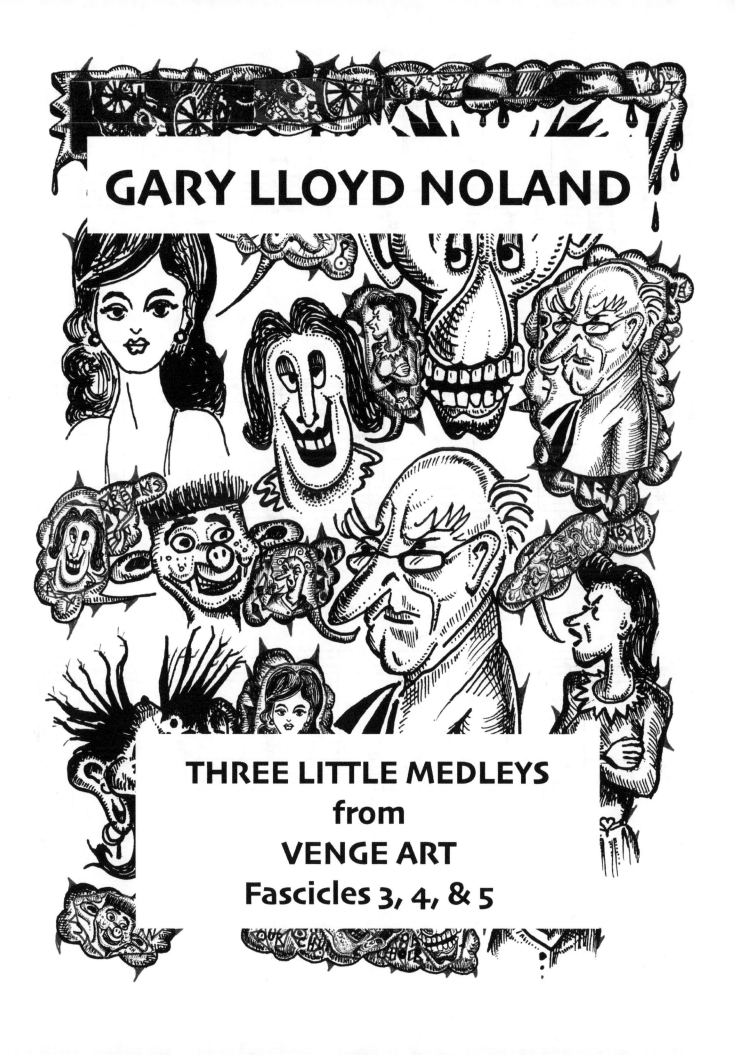

GARY LLOYD NOLAND

THREE LITTLE MEDLEYS
from
VENGE ART
Fascicles 3, 4, & 5

(Sonata for piano Op. 111 by Beethoven)   (Intermezzo Op. 119, No. 2 by Brahms)

(Also sprach Zarathustra Op. 30 by Richard Strauss)   (Kindertotenlieder by Gustav Mahler)

(Klavierstück Op. 33a by Arnold Schoenberg)

(Fugue No. 21 from The Well-Tempered Clavier, Book 1 by J.S. Bach)

(Piano Sonata No. 13 in B flat Major, K.333, 3. Allegretto grazioso, by Mozart)

(Intermezzo in B-Flat Major, Op. 76, No. 4 by Brahms)

(Till Eulenspiegels lustige Streiche, Op. 28, by Richard Strauss)

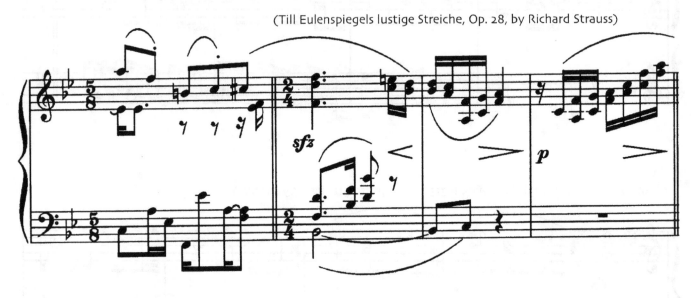

(Piano Sonata No. 1, 1. Allegro non troppo, by Erich Wolfgang Korngold)

Andante cantabile

(Intermezzo for string quartet by Hugo Wolf)

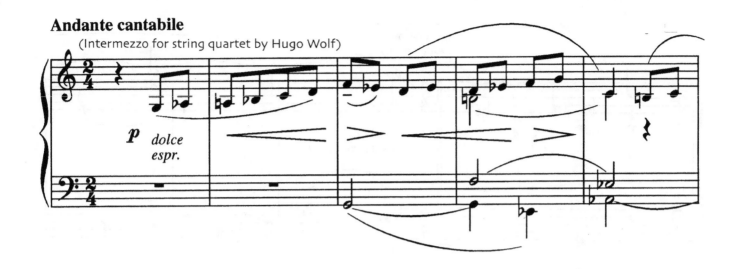

(Romance for violin & piano Op. 23
by Karol Szymanowski)

(Piano Sonata Op. 1
by Alban Berg)

(Adagio from Symphony 10 by Gustav Mahler)

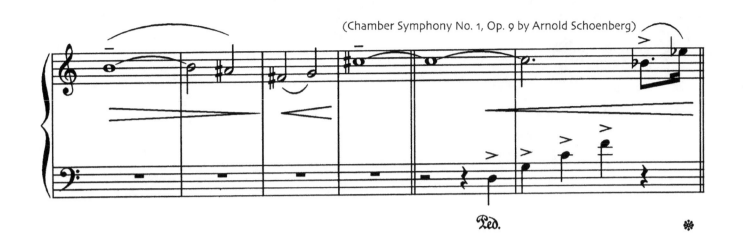

(Chamber Symphony No. 1, Op. 9 by Arnold Schoenberg)

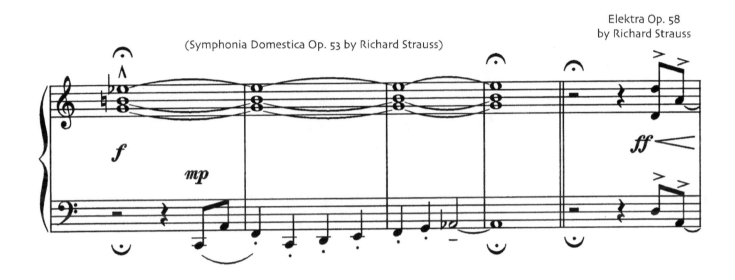

(Symphonia Domestica Op. 53 by Richard Strauss)

Elektra Op. 58
by Richard Strauss

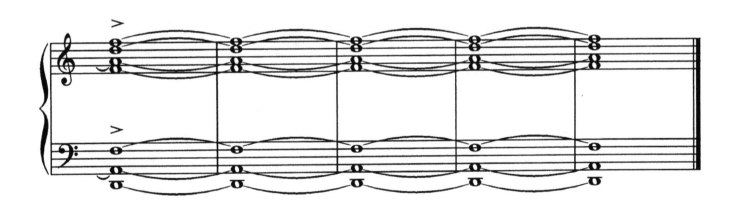

GARY LLOYD NOLAND

THREE INCONGRUISMS

for piano

Op. 122

1. Gottes Sohn ist kommen

a Chorale Prelude for piano

based on J.S. Bach's Choralgesang B. A. 39, No. 65 (Michael Weisse 1531)

Gary Lloyd Noland, Op. 122, No. 1
(1976-77, rev. 2021)

Lento religioso

molto espressivo

2. Fantasia
for piano

Gary Noland, Op. 122, No. 2

Andante moderato, maestoso

3. ALSO SPRACH MARGINMAN
for piano

Gary lloyd Noland, Op. 122, No. 3

Allegretto, distilled, abstract, cerebral: with precision and refinement

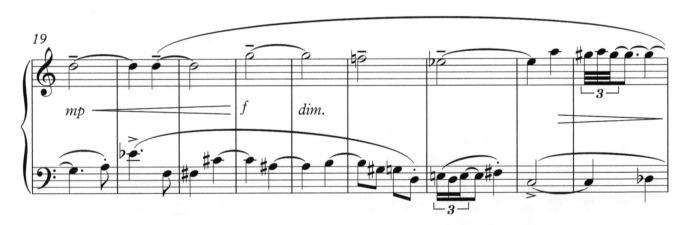

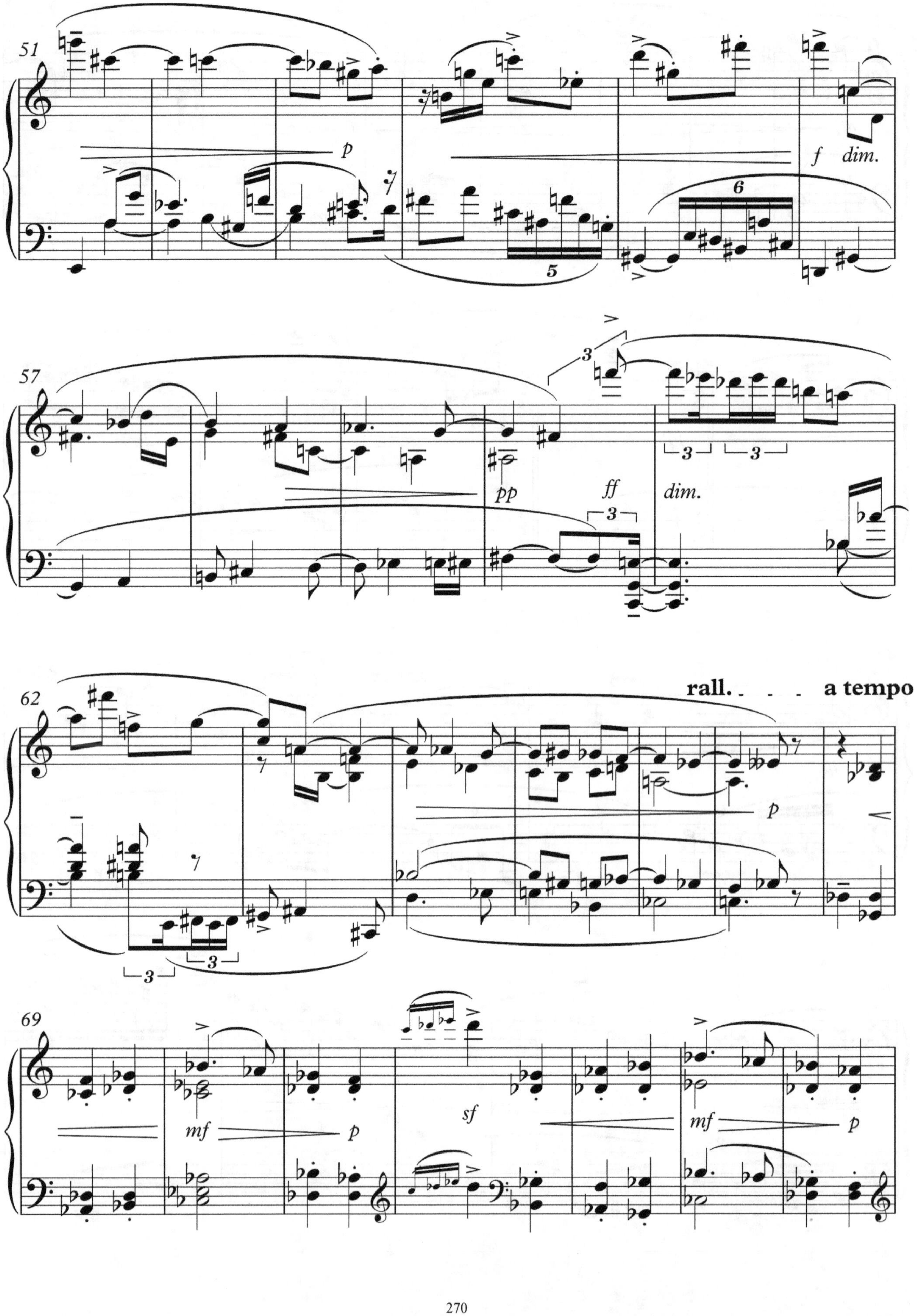
51
p
f
dim.
57
pp
ff
dim.
62
rall.
a tempo
p
69
mf
p
sf
mf
p

ABOUT THE COMPOSER

Short Bio (First Person)

I grew up in a headbox as an airhole freak, soliciting gestural acknowledgments of edibility crapropos of my monthly grub. The greenish gruel I ingested for nourishment drizzled in daggers from the broad vicinity of the ropemaster's, the driller's, and the eggman's quarters high aloft in the west-facing sumpwing of my cloaca maxima. I'd wile away my weeks watching ratsnakes swabbling down the dried up, crusty accounts off the edge of the slop pail in which I inveterately soaked my false tooth.

Long Bio (Third Person)

GARY LLOYD NOLAND (a.k.a. author **DOLLY GRAY LANDON**, visual artist **LON GAYLORD DYLAN**, and musicians **ARNOLD DAY LONGLY, ORLAN DOY GLANDLY** & **DARNOLD OLLY YANG**) was born in Seattle in 1957 and grew up in a broken home in a crowded house shared by ten or more people on a plot of land three blocks south of UC Berkeley known as People's Park, which has distinguished itself as a site of civil unrest since the late 1960s. As an adolescent, Noland lived for a time in Salzburg (Mozart's birthplace) and Garmisch-Partenkirchen (home of Richard Strauss), where he absorbed a host of musical influences. Having studied with a long roster of acclaimed composers and musicians, he earned a Bachelor's degree in music from UC Berkeley in 1979, continued his studies at the Boston Conservatory, and transferred to Harvard University, where he added to his credits a Masters and a PhD in Music Composition in 1989. His teachers in composition and theory have included John Clement Adams (not to be confounded with composers John Coolidge Adams or John Luther Adams), Alan Curtis (harpsichordist, musicologist, conductor, and one of the musical "stars" in Werner Herzog's film on Gesualdo, "Death for Five Voices"), Sir Peter Maxwell Davies (Master of the Queen's Music from 2004-16), William Denny (student of Paul Dukas), Robert Dickow, Janice Giteck (student of Darius Milhaud and Olivier Messiaen), Andrew Imbrie (student of Nadia Boulanger and Roger Sessions, Pulitzer Prize Finalist, 1995), Earl Kim (student of Arnold Schoenberg, Ernest Bloch, and Roger Sessions), Leon Kirchner (student of Arnold Schoenberg and assistant to Ernest Bloch and Roger Sessions, Pulitzer Prize, 1967) David Lewin (dubbed "the most original and far-ranging theorist of his generation"), Donald Martino (student of Milton Babbitt, Roger Sessions, and Luigi Dallapiccola, Pulitzer Prize, 1974), Hugo Norden, Marta Ptaszynska (student of Nadia Boulanger and Olivier Messiaen), Chris Rozé (student of Charles Wuorinen, Ursula Mamlok, and Vincent Persichetti), Goodwin Sammel (student of pianist Claudio Arrau), John Swackhamer (student of Ernst Krenek and Roger Sessions), Ivan Tcherepnin (student of Pierre Boulez and Karlheinz Stockhausen, son of Alexander Tcherepnin), and Walter Winslow (brother of Portland composer Jeff Winslow). Noland has attended seminars by composers David Del Tredici (Pulitzer Prize, 1980), Beverly Grigsby (student of Ernst Krenek), Michael Finnissy (leading British composer and pianist), and Bernard Rands (Pulitzer Prize, 1984), and has had private consultations with George Rochberg ("Father of Neo-Romanticism," Pulitzer Prize finalist, 1986) and Joaquin Nin-Culmell (student of Paul Dukas and Manuel de Falla, brother of essayist and diarist Anaïs Nin).

To continue on with this (undoubtedly tasteless to some) name-dropping pageant, Noland has also had the honor of meeting (howsoever briefly) such luminaries as Lukas Foss (who was highly supportive of him and with whom he maintained a brief correspondence), Elliot Carter, George Crumb, Frederic Rzewski, John Adams, Virgil Thomson, Oswald Jonas (student of Heinrich Schenker, founder of the Schenker Institut), John Corigliano, Stephen Hough, Henry Martin (composer of "WTC III"), Tison Street, Gunther Schuller, John Harbison, Peter Lieberson (five-time Pulitzer Prize finalist and son of the former president of Columbia Records Goddard Lieberson), Lina Prokofiev (wife of Sergei Prokofiev, with whom Noland once had a brief afternoon tête-à-tête), Sir Peter Pears (the English tenor whose career was long associated with that of composer Benjamin Britten), English mezzo-soprano Dame Janet Baker, Alvin Curran, Charles Amirkhanian, Marc-André Hamelin, Gyorgi Ligeti, Hsueh-Yung Shen (composer and percussionist extraordinaire, student of Nadia Boulanger, Darius Milhaud, and Lukas Foss), John Zorn (under whose baton he once performed), Noam Elkies (leading Harvard mathematician and composer), Robert Levin, Tomas Svoboda, and (thru correspondence): Joseph Fennimore, Ladislav Kupkovic, William Bolcom, Max Morath, and others. He also found himself on various occasions within spitting reach of (though didn't quite have the chutzpah at the time to waylay) composers Olivier Messiaen, John Cage, Arvo Pärt, Alfred Schnittke, Hans Werner Henze, William Albright, Brian Ferneyhough, Leslie Bassett, Luciano Berio (next to whom he once sat at a concert), Milton Babbitt, John Williams, Pierre Boulez, John McCabe, and others. In the early 1990's Noland used to dine with a friend of his grandmother's who recounted the story of having once met Gustav Mahler and Bruno Walter while on a hike in the hills outside of Vienna. On the darker side, Noland once met a woman in Cambridge who recounted having attended parties hosted by government officials in Berlin as a young girl in the 1930s where she witnessed her mother (whose husband was an ambassador representing a neutral Latin American country at the time) dancing with none other than (blech!) Adolf Hitler, who had been on friendly terms with descendants of Richard Wagner. Noland's maternal grandparents, who, along with his mother and uncle, fled the Nazis in 1936, recounted how they would often see Einstein (who knew Leopold Godowsky and Arnold Schoenberg) stroll past their home in Berlin back in the 1920s and early 1930s. (*Und so weiter und so fort...*)

One can go on and on recounting other historical connections, interlinkages, and associations Noland has had with famous and important musicians and non-musicians alike. This is not meant in any way, shape, or form to reflect favorably (or, for that matter, unfavorably) upon Noland's own creative endeavors but only as testimony to how privileged he has been (for which he is eternally grateful) to have either met and/or to have been in close proximity to such a legion of distinguished, powerful, and influential luminaries. To those readers who are easily offended by (and/or are inclined to view) this autobiographical account as being blatantly disingenuous and/or self-aggrandizing in tone, the composer offers his semi-sincere condolences for what may, not unforeseeably, smack of shameless name-dropping. One needs must admit, howso, that such shoulder-rubbings as hereinbefore described are highly instructive insofar as shedding light upon the streams of musico-artistic influences that are paramountly important in consideration of how they tend to impact, and ultimately lend cohesion and coherence to, the sum and substance of a composer's creative oeuvre. This is by no means out of the ordinary, for the power of such lineal influences upon artists is empirically universal—they all tend to eat off of one another's plates. There are deep cultural, historical, and psychological explanations (call them "roots" if thou wilt) as to why a composer writes a specific kind of music, and his or her reasons for doing so are less a matter of choice than due to some overpowering inner compulsion over which he or she has only the minutest modicum of self-control. Multiple attempts have been made (by critics and others) to pigeonhole Noland into some pre-defined aesthetic category or school of thought. As a composer, he has often been (mis)labeled as "avant-garde," "neo-romantic," "neo-classical," "modernist," "minimalist," "maximalist,' "postmodern," "radical," "reactionary," "tonal," "atonal," "dadaist," "romantic," "neo-baroque," and/or "iconoclastic" (among other things). None of these tags or isms, in and of themselves, are adequate to describe who he is or what he does (even the charge of iconoclasticism is a bit skewed), and most of these applied logos are not only functionally irrelevant but consummately meaningless. The composer eschews such classifications, since the affixtures of such generic diagnostic labels to one's body of work can prove immensely misleading to an otherwise grossly misinformed public at large. One need only instance what is known as the "Bolero Syndrome" to back up this point, lest there be any bones of contention thereanent, for howsoever adventitious such typecasting may be, it nurtures the inherent potentiality of damnifying a composer's reputability, especially amongst his or her peers of the musical realm. Noland's music has drawn innumerable comparisons (and fomblitudes) to a wide range of compositional influences, including music by composers as sundry and divers as the likes of Richard Strauss, John Cage, Frederic Chopin, Karlheinz Stockhausen, J.S. Bach, Robert Schumann, John Zorn, Max Reger, W. A. Mozart, Olivier Messiaen, Edward Elgar, Franz Schubert, Frederic Rzewski, George Rochberg, Conlon Nancarrow, Frank Zappa, Scott Joplin, Charles Ives, Ludwig van Beethoven, Cecil Taylor, John Dowland, Thelonius Monk, Johannes Brahms, Arnold Schönberg, Phillip Glass, Gustav Mahler, Erik Satie, and many others. A marked preponderance of such similitudinizations rings, perhaps, with occasional discrete elements of truth (and is, nevertheless, not unflattering to the recipient thereof, as such comparisons can in most cases be taken as encomiums) but none of these things even marginally suffice to tell the story of who the composer is, what his most matterable and momentous accomplishments are, why he writes the kind of music he does, or what his compositions signify in connection with the historical context(s) in which they are produced.

One can only hope against all hopes that, in virtue of the all-pervasive corruption and depravity distinguishing the bureaucrappic abomination that, until only a few short months ago (at the time of this writing), wielded its rubber fists unrelentingly over the politico-moral ideologies of the swank-and-vile for the purpose of breeding a veritable death cult inwith the bottommost echelons of its schlubordinate ranks (namely: those who would, according to its pre-calculatory caballings, be totalitarianly rightwashed into obsequiously serving not just the baby-fingered monster's pecuniary but also its hell-fired ego-bloating exigencies), as betwixt and betweentimes it empowers, and therewith imbibulates, its fetid effluvium to permeate each and every constituent element of the existing sociocultural milieu—Dandies & Gentledames: welcome to the COVID era!—'twould in a slump be perceived, by those possessing even the paltriest iota of hypo-critical acumen, as a perfectly natural outcome of the ubiquitous surfeit of ignormation and improperganda coupled with the complexity of kinks and viewpoints that have evolved as a result of the chaotic musical landscape that has emerged in recent quinquennia (not to fight shy of unmentioning the multiplicity of dinfluences, once accessible only to the topmost echelons of the eggheaded elite, that has been globally disseminated by dint of an ultroneous cross-pollination of diverse and powerful artistic lineages, as well as the commingling and interfusing of snub-cultures, past and present alike), which may well serve to impact, and ultimately lend a sort of structural cohesion (assuming that such a phenomenon is not pre-indisposed to be steemed a desirable asset inwith the prevailing ethico-moral codes of the present frivolizational ethos) to an artist's creative output (presupposing overmore that the artist under scrutiny is a thinking individual who has achieved a markedly eminent plateau of craftsmanly adroitness), that one's critical response thereto would, at an irreducible minimum, be that of paying a fitting tribute (insofar as putting one's celery where one's mouth is, that is) by granting formal agnition (even though in all likelihood "too-little-toolate," having been mongo decenniums overdue) to the creative outpourings (whether willful on the part of the perpetrator or no) as being LEGIT, AUTHENTIC and/or preeminently AUTHORITATIVE works of artistic expression.

To polemicize, hammergag, or stupinionate obstreperously to the contrary—that is, insofar as afforcing to delegitimize the brainchildren of unexceptionably accomplished creators by virtue of the convenient dismission of their effections in the vein of stigmatizing them for manifesting uncorroborated mouthprints of "derivativeness," "historicism," "pastiche" and suchlike (hackneyed forms of faultfinding, accidentarily, that have in due season come to represent the stereotypical tropes that have, time out of number, been shown to possess an instinctible propensity for oozing their way diarrhoeically from the hollowed, sphinct-like groves of vainstream cacademe, and the formalistically run-of-the-drill, accreditated musics of which have also not unfailed to disprove, over and again, to have scarce if any shelf-life in the unadulterated domain of contemporary classical ear-meat manufacturing)—would be either disingenuous, naïve, or dazzlingly indolent on the part of the criticasters under scrutiny.

Far offshore as it might seem, it has come to this dotmaker's attention, thru empirical observations conducted over a quaternity of decades, that 'tis often-whiles not unprone to be the case that the more refined, facete, and scrupulously rigorous the caliber of the craftsmanship and artistry of a given musical production is fair to be—and one oughtn't make any bones about the effect that stylistic distinctiveness per se is all but impossimaginable without a composer achieving a consummate mastery of his or her art (a truism powered by ample historical evidence)—the more probable it is that charges of "pastiche" and other opprobrious, derogatory abusions will be leveled against said composer by invidious flubdubs, ableless wannabes, affectatious morons, conceited simpletons, pompous nincompoops, impenitent philistines, and ladders of other insufferably bombastic socialclimbing snoots, parasites, toadies, and other bottom-feeding intestinal cack-weasels, microbes, barnacles, maggots, and the like. There is no "straight and narrow" in the art of music creation—it is an indescribably messy and chaotic affair that necessitates a fierce, sustained, and uncompromising focus of fanatically devoted attention and feverish concentration, never mind a preternatural willingness to have the mockers put on one's dignity and through-bearing, even to the point, perforce, of dicing with one's very own death. One of Noland's self-coined aphorisms is: "There are no rules in love, war, and art." Another, based upon an inversion of filmmaker Luis Buñuel's celebrious quism, reads: "Art without craft is like salt without an egg."

Gary Lloyd Noland's ever-expanding catalogue consists of scores of opuses, which include piano, vocal, chamber, orchestral, experimental, and electronic pieces, full-length plays in verse, "chamber novels," and graphically notated scores. His critically acclaimed, award-winning 77-hour long *Gesamtkunstwerk* JAGDLIED: a Chamber Novel for Narrator, Musicians, Pantomimists, Dancers & Culinary Artists (Op. 20) was listed by one reviewer as the Number

One book of 2018. His "39 Variations on an Original Theme in F Major" for solo piano Op. 98 (included in this collection) is, at approximately two hours duration, one of the lengthiest and most challenging sets of solo piano variations in the history of the genre. It has been called by American composer Ernesto Ferreri "an historical variation set for piano, a true descendant of the Goldbergs and Diabellis, beautifully targeted to an apotheosis of supreme grandeur." Composer/pianist Ludwig Tuman described it as "an astounding tour de force. In its far-reaching, systematic exploration of the theme's creative possibilities, as well as in the inexhaustible imagination brought to bear, it reminds one of the Goldberg and the Diabelli. But in its monumental dimensions it goes far beyond them both, and in the large number of historical styles referenced and integrated into the work … I am unaware of any parallel. I especially enjoyed the consistent use of certain features of the theme, regardless of the style or the type of tonality, pantonality or atonality employed—among them the melodic turn, the phrases ascending by whole steps, and others. I offer my humble congratulations on a titanic achievement!"

Having received both effusive praise and violent censure of his music over the years, Noland has been called "the Richard Strauss of the 21st century," "the [Max] Reger of the 21st century," "the most prominent American composer (of modern classical music) of our times," "the most virtuosic composer of fugue alive today," "the composer to end all composers," "court jester to the classical establishment," and "one of the great composers of the 21st century," and has on numerous occasions been branded a "genius." He has also been called some pretty colorful names by his detractors—names unsuitable for publication in the pages of this volume. Although the composer feels something of a constitutional disinclination to share with his prospective groupies the aforesaid hyperbolical quotations, as it causes him (howsoever unwittingly) to mount a red flag, he is clevertheless all but compelled to trumpet such encomiums for the sake of ensuring his survival in the present-day blaringly obnoxious, braggadocious milieu, notwithgrandstanding that he is neither flannelmouthed nor overweening by nature but— quite *au contraire*—of a singularly equanimous poise and disposition. Unfreely farouche and retiring by nature, composer Noland is, by his own admission (and, beyond peradventure, to his ultimate detriment) an ineradicably head-in-the-clouds introvert par *excellence*.

Noland's compositions have been performed and broadcast (including on NPR) in many locations throughout the United States, as well as in Europe, Asia, and Australia. His music has also been heard on six continents via various music-streaming platforms. Noland founded the Seventh Species Contemporary Classical Music Concert Series in San Francisco in 1990 and has, since, produced upwards of fifty-plus concerts of contemporary classical music on the West Coast. He is also a founding member of Cascadia Composers, which has, since the time of its inception in 2008, mushroomed into a veritable colossus of an organization supporting regional and national composers, as well as performers of contemporary classical music, and has, furtherover, distinguished itself as one of the premier collectives of its kind on the West Coast. Noland has taught music at Harvard, the University of Oregon, and a couple of community colleges (bleah!), and currently teaches piano, theory, and composition as a private independent instructor in the Portland, Oregon metro area.

A number of Noland's works (fiction, music, and graphic scores) have been published (and/or are slated for publication) in various litmags, including Quarter After Eight, Berkeley Fiction Review, Portland Review, Denali, The Monarch Review, Prick of the Spindle, theNewerYork Press, Wisconsin Review, The Writing Disorder, and Heavy Feather Review. His graphic scores are included in Theresa Sauer's book NOTATIONS 21 (2009), which is a sequel to John Cage's celebrated compilation of graphic scores: NOTATIONS (first published in 1969). A chapter on Noland is included in Burl Willes's celebrated book TALES FROM THE ELMWOOD: A COMMUNITY MEMORY published by the Berkeley Historical Society in 2000. In 1999 Noland was awarded the Oregon Composer of the Year Award jointly by the Oregon Music Teachers Association (OMTA) and Music Teachers National Association (MTNA) and was commissioned to compose his SEPTET for clarinet, saxophone, French horn, two violins, double bass, and piano (Op. 43). Noland's GRANDE RAG BRILLANTE Op. 15 (included in this collection) was commissioned by KPFA Radio to celebrate the inauguration of its (then, in 1991) brand new Pacifica Radio Headquarters in Berkeley. This premiere was later acknowledged in Nicolas Slonimsky's book MUSIC SINCE 1900.

Many of Noland's scores are available from J.W. Pepper, RGM, Sheet Music Plus, and Freeland Publications. Six CDs of his compositions are available on the North Pacific Music label at northpacificmusic.com. Nine more new CDs of his compositions will be made available in the near future. Over 400 videos and audio recordings of Noland's music and narratives are available for listening and viewing on YouTube, Vimeo, Soundcloud, Spotify, Apple Music, Amazon Music, Pandora and hosts of other music streaming networks worldwide. Most of Noland's music videos and audio recordings are also available for viewing and listening on his website: http://www.composergarynoland.godaddysites.com/

Noland's COLLECTED PIANO WORKS: Volume 1 is available for purchase at many major book retailers worldwide. Here is the Amazon link at which it can be ordered: https://www.amazon.com/Collected-Piano-Works-Lloyd-Noland/dp/1732302383/ref=asc_df_1732302383/?tag=hyprod-20&linkCode=df0&hvadid=539702681678&hvpos=&hvnetw=g&hvrand=15835365890307304374&hvpone=&hvptwo=&hvqmt=&hvdev=c&hvdvcmdl=&hvlocint=&hvlocphy=9032854&hvtargid=pla-1412571247136&psc=1

Noland's award-winning chamber novel JAGDLIED is currently available for purchase at: https://www.amazon.com/gp/product/B07GJ1RDQJ?pf_rd_p=183f5289-9dc0-416f-942e-e8f213ef368b&pf_rd_r=FJW5GVTYY1NKTJ47M5B5

Noland's critically acclaimed six-hour play NOTHING IS MORE: A HIGH BLACK COMEDY IN VERSE WITH MUSIC FOR SIX ACTORS is available for purchase at: https://www.amazon.com/Nothing-More-Black-Comedy-Actors/dp/1795387513/ref=tmm_pap_swatch_0?_encodi